I0159553

The Manhood and Deity of Christ

James Mead

ISBN: 978-1-78364-515-2

www.obt.org.uk

****

The Open Bible Trust
Fordland Mount, Upper Basildon,
Reading, RG8 8LU, UK.

The Manhood and Deity of Christ

Contents

1.
Introduction

1. Introduction

The Incarnation of Christ (and some have called it a "mystery") is one of the foundation blocks of our faith. It is an "essential" if we are to understand the purposes of God from Creation to future glory in His presence.

But it is, for many people, a huge stumbling block, sometimes preventing them from coming to believe the Christian message because it undoubtedly challenges our minds and perceptions of our earth-bound reality. Does that mean that, as Christians, we understand it? Charles Wesley couldn't have put it any better when he penned a hymn which begins:

> Let earth and Heaven combine,
> Angels and men agree,
> To praise in songs divine
> The incarnate Deity,
> Our God contracted to a span,
> Incomprehensibly made man.

He is right – the incarnation is "incomprehensible". We are finite beings and no matter how much new knowledge scientific research has uncovered about the mysteries of the brain, no matter how much psychological research has added to our knowledge of the mind, there is a limit to our understanding of the great questions in life. So how are we to approach the incarnation of Christ without getting into a spiritual and intellectual muddle? Initially, if we are honest, with great difficulty! All we can do is to explore Scripture and pray that the Holy Spirit will minister and enlighten the Word to us. I'm not out to "prove" the incarnation. As Christians we embrace the wonderful consequences of it while, at the same time, accepting its incomprehensibility, or mystery, as some commentators write.

2.

Manhood

2. Manhood

Meekness and Majesty
Manhood and Deity,
In perfect harmony,
The Man who is God.
Lord of eternity
Dwells in humanity,
Kneels in humility
And washes our feet.

> *O what a mystery,*
> *Meekness and majesty.*
> *Bow down and worship*
> *For this is your God,*
> *This is your God.*

Look up the word "manhood" in Scripture and you will not find it. Graham Kendrick's lyrics for his song above are only his way of expressing Scripture in song; a poet's version if you like. So let us look at a few references to the word "man" and explore the truths behind them.

We can begin at the beginning in Genesis:

> Then God said, "Let us make mankind in our image, in our likeness, so that they may rule over the fish in the sea and the birds in the sky, over the livestock and all the wild animals, and over all the creatures that move along the ground." (Genesis 1:26)

The word for "man", or "mankind" as it is here, is the Hebrew *adam*. So it has a singular and a collective meaning. Here it has the collective meaning and it is telling us in a general statement that God created mankind. When we go to chapter 2 we move from the general to the particular:

> The LORD God formed the man from the dust of the ground and breathed into his nostrils the breath of life, and the man became a living being. (Genesis 2:7)

The word "man" is *adam* and it is singular. The man was formed from the dust of the ground; he was of the earth. Now let us turn to Paul's letter to the Corinthians:

The first man was of the dust of the earth; the second man of heaven. (1 Corinthians 15:47)

The Greek word for "man" in both cases in this verse is the same. It is *anthropos* meaning "one of the human race" and the Greek *anthropos* is equivalent to the Hebrew *adam*. So we have an exact identification here; both the first Adam and the second Adam are the same in this respect. What differentiates them is the origin. The first Adam is "out of" the earth (Greek *ek*), the second Adam is "of" heaven (Greek *ex*). The first Adam was "made"; the second Adam simply "is".

Just before that passage, in verse 21, Paul wrote:

For since death came through a man, the resurrection of the dead comes also through a man. (1 Corinthians 15:21)

Once again the word for "man" is the same in both cases (Greek *anthropos* - one of the human race).

Then, in his first letter to Timothy, Paul states:

> For there is one God and one mediator
> between God and men, the man Christ Jesus.
> (1 Timothy 2:5)

The Greek for "one" is an emphatic word and it means "one which excludes all others". It is unapologetically exclusive for it has echoes of John 14 when Jesus said that "no one comes to the Father except by me" (verse 6) and also of the sermon after Pentecost where Peter said that "there is no other name under heaven given to men by which we must be saved" (Acts 4:12). There is only one way to the Father and only one way of Salvation, but it is open to all who will respond; in this sense it is inclusive.

The Greek word "mediator" is *mesites*. It means a "go-between". Here it means "one who mediates between two parties with a view to producing peace." Vine adds to this when he writes:

> ... more than mere mediatorship is in view,
> for the salvation of men necessitated that the

Mediator should Himself possess the nature and attributes of Him TOWARDS whom He acts, and should likewise participate in the nature of those FOR WHOM He acts (sin apart) ... Only by being possessed both of Deity and humanity could He comprehend the CLAIMS of the one and the NEEDS of the other. (W E Vine; *The Expository Dictionary of New Testament Words)*

And the word for "man" (in 1 Timothy 2:5) is, once again, *anthropos* - one of the human race.

This is what John writes when Jesus was brought before the people by Pilate:

> Pilate came out again and said to them, "Behold, I am bringing Him out to you so that you may know that I find no guilt in Him." Jesus then came out, wearing the crown of thorns and the purple robe. Pilate said to them, "Behold the Man!" So when the chief priests and the officers saw Him, they cried out saying, "Crucify, crucify!" Pilate said to them, "Take Him yourselves

and crucify Him, for I find no guilt in Him.".
(John 19:4-6)

The Greek for man is, again, *anthropos*. What the people saw was a man who had been flogged, abused and was bleeding. But it was a man presented as a defeated king. It was a cruel mockery of a king's authority, for here was a king with a robe and a crown but with no power. Here was a seemingly defeated man.

One of the key passages is the great chapter 2 in Philippians;

> Who, being in very nature God, did not consider equality with God something to be used to his own advantage; rather, he made himself nothing by taking the very nature of a servant, being made in human likeness. And being found in appearance as a man, he humbled himself by becoming obedient to death - even death on a cross! (Philippians 2:6-8)

The Greek word translated "nature" in verse 6 is *morphe* which means:

> properly, *form* (outward expression) that *embodies essential* (inner) substance so that the *form* is in complete harmony with the inner *essence*.

"in appearance" is the Greek *schema* and it means:

> properly, *exterior* shape (form); (figuratively) *the outer "shape"* (*manner, appearance*).

> *schēma* ("outward, visible form") is used of Jesus' earthly body (Philippian 2:7,8). (Strong; *Concordance with Hebrew, Chaldee and Greek Dictionaries*)

Christ was incarnated into a *genuine physical* body, which was not an "exact match with typical humanity" because His body was *never touched or tainted by sin* (even original sin).

Herein lies another great mystery; Christ was sinless. So it begs the question "How can He be truly human for we are all tainted with the sin of Adam?" Surely the amazing and incomprehensible answer is in Corinthians:

> God made him who had no sin to be sin for us, so that in him we might become the righteousness of God. (2 Corinthians 5:21)

This must be one of the most remarkable verses in Scripture for it underlines both the divinity and the humanity of Jesus. When we look at the cross we see a man. All men die and we see a man dying. All men sin and we see a man who *became* sin; who was identified completely with sin which, as Paul points out in Romans 6:23, results in death.

An old Commentator puts it this way:

> The train of thought is that God dealt with Christ, not as though He were a sinner, like other men, but as though He were sin itself, absolutely identified with it. (Ellicott;

Commentary for English Reader: 2 Corinthians 5:21)

Hence the heart-rending cry from the cross: "My God, my God. Why have your forsaken me?" (Matthew 27:46). God not only turned His back on His Son, but demonstrated His holiness by turning His back on Sin itself, for at Calvary Christ was made to be sin for us (see 2 Corinthians 5:21 quoted above). The hymn writer, C Austin Miles, gave a personal response to this:

They nailed my Lord upon the tree
And left Him, dying, there:
Thro' love he suffered there for me;
'Twas love beyond compare.

Crucified! Crucified!
And nailed upon the tree!
With piercéd hands and feet and side!
For you! For me!

Upon his head a crown of thorns,
Upon his heart my shame;
For me he prayed, for me he died,
And, dying, spoke my blame. [Refrain]

"Forgive them, O forgive!" he cried
Then bowed his sacred head;
"O Lamb of God! my sacrifice!"
For me thy blood was shed. [Refrain]

His voice I hear, tis love I know;
I worship at his feet;
And kneeling there, at Calv'ry's cross,
Redemption is complete. [Refrain]

The subsequent and triumphant resurrection, therefore, brings us to the Deity of Christ.

3.
Deity

3. Deity

There can be no more important passage than the opening verses of John 1.

> In the beginning was the Word, and the Word was with God, and the Word was God. He was in the beginning with God. All things came into being through Him, and apart from Him nothing came into being that has come into being. In Him was life, and the life was the Light of men. The Light shines in the darkness, and the darkness did not comprehend it.

There is so much here that it's impossible to explore it now, but the great word *logos* doesn't just mean "word" in the grammatical sense. It involves thought and ideas, statements and speeches. In fact it is language itself and therefore meaning and intention; further than that it is the very mind of God Himself.

It is quite obviously John's intention to echo the opening words of Genesis 1. There the act of creation originates from the mind of God and we read of the word of God being spoken: "And God said ..."

John doesn't give us a philosophical discourse as the Greeks would have loved. Instead he makes a series of statements whose implications are enormous.

- The Word was WITH God.
- The Word WAS God.
- The Word was there at the beginning of time and before that.
- The Word was the agent of Creation.
- The Word was life.
- The Word was light.

But when John wrote verse 14 it was an explosive statement which challenged the Greeks who were so fond of philosophical discussion (e.g. Paul in Athens in Acts 17). And it also challenged the

Jewish readers who, as Matthew wrote throughout his gospel, were looking for signs and wonders.

> And the Word became flesh and dwelt among us. (John 1:14)

This Word, this Logos, who wasn't just **with** God but **was** God, became a man. John had no doubt at all about who Jesus was; He was both fully God and fully human. How amazing is that? And furthermore the "darkness" of sin could do nothing about it.

Even His disciples struggled to comprehend who Jesus was. Remember the reaction of the disciples in the boat after the storm:

> The men were amazed and asked, "What kind of man is this? Even the winds and the waves obey him!" (Matthew 8:27)

Of course the winds and the waves obeyed Him because here was the Word without whom nothing would have been made. Here was the Creator

Himself controlling His creation. No wonder the disciples were amazed.

Throughout His life there were things which Jesus said that were quite explicit about His relationship with God.

The "I am" sayings in John's Gospel link Him with the revelation God gave to Moses:

> God said to Moses, "I AM WHO I AM. This is what you are to say to the Israelites: 'I AM has sent me to you.'" (Exodus 3:14)

When Jesus said "*I am* the resurrection and the life" … here was the Word, who was with God and who was God, speaking words of life. In Jesus the I AM of Exodus wasn't sending anyone else to make the sacrifice for sin … the I AM came Himself.

John records that Jesus said:

> "I and the Father are one." (John 10:30)

The word "one" here means "one in will and in spirit." Jesus said that He had come to do the will of His Father because Jesus' will was exactly and completely identified with the Father's.

Paul wrote these magnificent words to the Colossian Church:

> The Son is the image of the invisible God, the firstborn over all creation. For in him all things were created: things in heaven and on earth, visible and invisible, whether thrones or powers or rulers or authorities; all things have been created through him and for him. He is before all things, and in him all things hold together. And he is the head of the body, the church; he is the beginning and the firstborn from among the dead, so that in everything he might have the supremacy. For God was pleased to have all his fullness dwell in him, and through him to reconcile to himself all things, whether things on earth or things in heaven, by making peace through his blood, shed on the cross. (Colossians 1:15-20)

The shedding of His blood underlines the humanity of Christ and the resurrection underlines the Deity of Christ.

The response of Thomas, his mind full of doubt and confusion, when confronted with the risen Lord Jesus, expresses a remarkable understanding. In front of him was …

- the Man whom he had followed for three years;
- the Man who had stilled the storm;
- the Man who had fed 5000 people;
- the Man who had been nailed to a cross;
- the Man who had died and been buried in a tomb.

When Thomas said simply, but with all his heart, "My Lord and my God!" (John 20:26-29), not only was it a deeply personal response ("my"), it was also a recognition of who Jesus – the Man who stood before him – was. The Greek for 'Lord' is *kyrios* and it has the meaning of 'Lord' in the sense of 'absolute ownership'. And the Greek for

'God' here is *theos*, which means the creator and sustainer of all things. Thomas' words were words of recognition and submission, for in that dramatic moment Thomas had grasped something of the mystery of the incarnation.

And if we think of events pertaining to His birth we read:

> All this took place to fulfil what the Lord had said through the prophet: "The virgin will conceive and give birth to a son, and they will call him Immanuel" (which means "God with us"). (Matthew 1:22,23)

In the stable, whatever form that took, was the Word, the Agent of Creation itself, the I AM that confronted Moses, the Mighty God of Isaiah 9:6. In that manger slept the Alpha and Omega, the First and the Last of Revelation. It held the Saviour, the Man of Sorrows of Isaiah 53, the sacrificial Lamb of God recognised by John as the one who would "take away the sin of the world" (John 1:29).

But, above all it held, in the words of Paul, the "Son of God who loved me and gave Himself for me" (Galatians 2:20). What greater truth can we rejoice in at Christmas when we remember His birth?

****

.

Let earth and Heaven combine,
Angels and men agree,
To praise in songs divine
The incarnate Deity,
Our God contracted to a span,
Incomprehensibly made man.

He laid His glory by,
He wrapped Him in our clay;
Unmarked by human eye,
The latent Godhead lay;
Infant of days He here became,
And bore the mild Immanuel's name.

See in that infant's face
The depths of deity,
And labour while ye gaze
To sound the mystery
In vain; ye angels gaze no more,
But fall, and silently adore.

Unsearchable the love
That hath the Saviour brought;
The grace is far above
Or men or angels' thought:
Suffice for us that God, we know,
Our God, is manifest below.

He deigns in flesh to appear,
Widest extremes to join;
To bring our vileness near,
And make us all divine:
And we the life of God shall know,
For God is manifest below.

Made perfect first in love,
And sanctified by grace,
We shall from earth remove,
And see His glorious face:
His love shall then be fully showed,
And man shall all be lost in God.

(Charles Wesley)

About the author

James Mead was born in 1950 in Dartford, Kent, and has been a "Dartfordian" ever since. He was educated at Dartford Grammar School before attending Avery Hill Teacher Training College and qualifying as a Primary teacher. He is also a musician and, while teaching, obtained a B. Mus. (Hons) from Goldsmith's College and later on a M.A. (Music in Education) from the Institute of Education, London University. He was a head teacher from 1990 to 2002 and then spent the final twelve years of his career teaching music in various local primary schools. He was also Music Director of the Kent County Junior Singers for 15 years. He now enjoys retirement and leads a Christian fellowship with his brother-in-law. He and his wife have two daughters and two grandchildren and they all live in Dartford.

Also on this subject

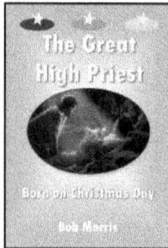
The Great High Priest
Born on Christmas Day
Bob Morris

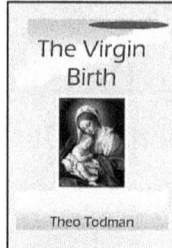
The Virgin Birth
Theo Todman

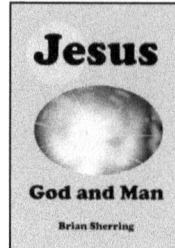
Jesus
God and Man
Brian Sherring

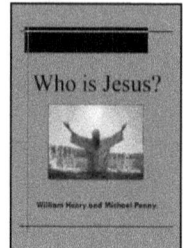
Who is Jesus?
William Henry and Michael Penny

Further details of the books on these pages can be seen on

www.obt.org.uk

The books are available from that website and from

The Open Bible Trust
Fordland Mount, Upper Basildon,
Reading, RG8 8LU, UK.

They are also available as eBooks from Amazon and Apple and as
KDP paperback from Amazon

The Great High Priest Born on Christmas Day
By Bob Morris

Just over 2,000 years ago, an angel of the Lord appeared in a dream to a man in Galilee named Joseph. He had just discovered that his fiancée was pregnant.

He was to learn that this Child was to be the Great High Priest in the Order of Melchizedek. As such He would be a sacrifice and a sympathiser, an intercessor and a mediator, and He was humanity's hope for the future, for eternal life.

The Virgin Birth
By Theo Todman

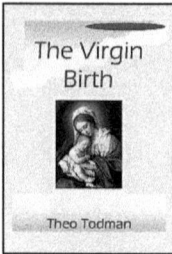

The reader will find in this publication a most stimulating and helpful presentation of the Scriptural teaching of *The Virgin Birth*. In small compass the author deals with:

- The major biblical passages;
- The theology of the Virgin Birth;
- The teaching of the early church; and
- Some alleged objections to the doctrine.

He also exposes many myths and misunderstanding.

Sufficient is given here to help the Christian understand the record of Scripture and emerge with a clearer understanding of the nature of Jesus Christ, the Son of God.

Who is Jesus?

By William Henry and Michael Penny

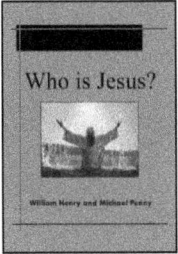

In Matthew 16:13-16 the Lord asked the disciples who the people said He was. What were their answers? Some answers were understandable, with a grain of truth, but none were correct. Then He turned to His disciples and asked them. What was their answer?

And what about today? Who do people, today, say Jesus is? Again, some of the answers from the man in the street may have a grain of truth, but how many people really know and appreciate who Jesus is? Do you? Who do you say that He is? What is your answer?

Jesus: God and Man
By Brian Sherring

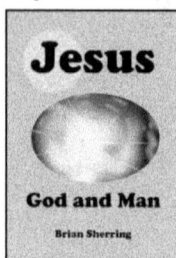

Whilst many Christians have no difficulty in accepting Jesus Christ as man, some do have problems believing that He is God. However, it is interesting to note that in the first century, the Gnostics did not question His deity: on the contrary, they questioned His humanity, for how could a man do what He did?

In this publication the author clearly sets out what the Scriptures say of Christ, about His being, His person.

Readers are encouraged to make up their own minds, but the volume of evidence presented here will lead the reader to appreciate why that sceptic of all sceptics, Thomas, cried out "My Lord and my God".

Further details of the books on these pages
can be seen on

www.obt.org.uk

The books are available from that website and
from

The Open Bible Trust
Fordland Mount, Upper Basildon,
Reading, RG8 8LU, UK.

They are also available as eBooks from Amazon
and Apple and as
KDP paperback from Amazon

Search magazine

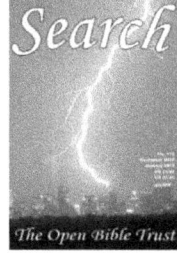

For a free sample of
the Open Bible Trust's magazine Search,
please email

admin@obt.org.uk

or visit

www.obt.org.uk/search

About this book

The Manhood and Deity of Christ

With a lovely combination of quotations from the Bible and verses from ancient hymns and modern songs, the author presents a perfect picture of that great mystery, the Incarnation—Christ who is both man and God. As Paul explained in Philippians 2: Jesus, although being in very nature God, took the very nature of a servant and was made human.

Publications of The Open Bible Trust must be in accordance with its evangelical, fundamental and dispensational basis. However, beyond this minimum, writers are free to express whatever beliefs they may have as their own understanding, provided that the aim in so doing is to further the object of The Open Bible Trust. A copy of the doctrinal basis is available on **www.obt.org.uk** or from:

THE OPEN BIBLE TRUST
Fordland Mount, Upper Basildon,
Reading, RG8 8LU, GB

www.ingramcontent.com/pod-product-compliance
Lightning Source LLC
Chambersburg PA
CBHW060628030426
42337CB00018B/3252